More Than My Skin

Why Being Black in America Is Hard

K. SADDLER

Fulton Books, Inc.
Meadville, PA

Published by Fulton Books 2020

ISBN 978-1-64952-241-2 (paperback)
ISBN 978-1-64952-242-9 (digital)

Printed in the United States of America

Contents

Acknowledgment

I first want to thank my Lord and savior because without him, I wouldn't have the strength to be the woman I am today. I want to acknowledge all of those that have suffered in this cruel world we live in because of the color of their skin. I am praying for all the families and mothers that have lost children because someone thought their skin tone made them different. To my ancestors and the leaders before my time, thank you! For the fight you gave to give us a chance at the little equality that does exist, due to your efforts and beliefs.

Introduction

Reflecting on everything that a biracial or African American goes through on a day to day basis is hard. I strongly believe that everyone should be treated equally, no matter their ethnicity. When I sit back and see all the hurtful events occurring daily between different races, police, and African Americans, it is an emotional thing to watch. I began to write my outlook and dealings that I, myself have dealt with and others around me. We need change and a fair way of life! All Americans should be treated based on their character as a human being, not the color of their skin. Our ancestors fought for our freedom, not for history to repeat itself, or mothers to fear their child will deal with hate crimes or death when they walk out of the house. For men to not get fair treatment within the system or have to deal with police brutality because they are black. We have voices and we want them heard!

Chapter 1

First, a Little History

For thousands of years, Black people were identified as slaves. We were captured from our homelands and imprisoned by Europeans and North Americans. We were uprooted from all that we knew; our identities were stripped from us. We were no longer seen as human beings but as commodities for trade and a means of cheap labor.

Our people were stripped of their dignity and humanity. We were seen as inferior, dirty, useless, ignorant, dumb, and many more degrading terms you can think of. We were painted with negativity and stereotypes that were invented just to keep us at the bottom of the totem pole, where our capturers believed we belonged.

Can you imagine a world where you are seen as a possession and not a human? That world was a reality for our forefathers. Slavery was introduced to the northern parts of the Americas in the 1600s, but by the 1800s, many states had abolished it after realizing how little of an impact it had on the economy. The American Revolution saw leaders in some states, realizing how their oppression of Africans was linked to their own oppression at the hands of the British.

Even though Congress outlawed the import of new slaves, slavery not only continued in the southern states, but it continued to increase as the years went by.

You see, as slaves, our people had no rights. We were regarded as the property of a slave master. The justice system was nonexistent in our case. Black people were treated with the utmost hatred and disgust; we endured the most inhumane of practices, and many of our people were murdered for simply wanting to be free.

Many antislavery advocates or abolitionists, such as Harriet Tubman and John Brown, created what was known as the underground railroad, which was a series of safe houses from the southern to the northern parts of America in which slaves would travel in order to be free. These abolitionists risked their lives for the freedom of many others but perished in the end.

The Union victory of the Civil War under the leadership of the antislavery president, Abraham Lincoln, millions of slaves were given freedom. However, this victory was incomplete. Even though Black people were free according to the law, they were severely restricted in all areas of life from education, funding, housing, employment, you name it.

Even though the Thirteenth Amendment abolished slavery in 1865, Black people were only considered as citizens after the Fourteenth Amendment, which was in 1868. This still did not garner afford them the right to vote. In fact, that only came in 1870 in the Fifteenth Amendment. All these victories did not bring much improvement to the social and economic situation that Black people were faced with. In many aspects, they were still slaves even though that title had been removed.

The impression was that Black people were free from oppression when, in actual fact, the form of oppression had just shifted. We were no longer physically oppressed but mentally, economically, and socially. We were told that we were equal, and yet the system continued to treat us as slaves. We were told that we were equal, and yet they created a divide, a distinction between us and themselves. Where was this freedom we were promised?

Segregation was the new form of slavery with the introduction of the "separate but equal" doctrine that took effect from 1896. This doctrine separated White people from Black people in every aspect of life. We were called citizens and had supposedly been given freedom, but segregation had ensured that our "freedom" had limitations.

The strongholds of slavery had taken form in segregation. Our minds had been imprisoned. We were stifled from achieving anything of significance. We were not offered any opportunities for self-improvement or empowerment; we became victims once again but in a different way. How are you supposed to live when your livelihood is limited?

Black people were stripped of everything and only given the bare minimum to survive because even though we were free on paper, we were not actually free. We couldn't go to the schools we wanted to, we couldn't live in the areas we wanted to, we couldn't dress the way we wanted to, we couldn't get the jobs we wanted, and we were banded together and trapped by the very system that declared us free.

In World War II, millions of Black people offered their lives to fight for their country, but even in that, the racism was as strong as ever. They offered their lives to fight for freedom that wasn't theirs.

This has been the unfortunate truth for Black people in America. We've been fighting a war our whole lives—fighting for freedom that we supposedly have but don't experience. Systems that were created thousands of years ago continue to work against us even to this day. We always have to go above and beyond just to prove ourselves—to prove our worth. We have been imprisoned by the very system that was supposed to be our savior.

Black tax, police brutality, unfair judgment, inequality, racism, segregation, prejudice, and many more are issues that African Americans continue to face to this day. So who said we were free? Why are we told to just accept our circumstances? Why are we supposed to be complacent when we barely have anything? Why should we go to bed at night grateful that we made it through the day? Why are we still oppressed? Aren't we human too?

Martin Luther King Jr.
Harriet Tubman
Crispus Attucks
Phyllis Wheatley
James Armistead Lafayette
Jackie Robinson
Rosa Parks
Malcolm X
Shirley Chisholm
Jesse Jackson
Marcus Garvey

And many others who fought and
paved the way for our freedom.

Chapter 2

I Am Not UglyBeauty Standards

What is beauty? What defines it? What does it look like? The subject of beauty is one that has always been a topic of discussion. We have seen how it evolves with time. But why doesn't this evolution ever favor those with darker skin? There are beauty standards that have been set by the world and pushed by media, but the interesting issue is that these standards are anti-Black. We now live in a world where the standard of beauty is long "tamed" hair, light skin, slim-toned figures that can rock a crop top. Now, from a genetic standpoint, African women usually have fuller, curvier figures. These body types went from being mocked and shamed to being fetished. Women of other races began to cosmetically enhance their bodies to resemble that of a full, curvy woman. There is no shame in plastic surgery, especially if you're unhappy with the way you look. The issue lies in that society does not associate Black people with beauty, and yet they want to look like us. This is, unfortunately, one of the greatest forms of oppression Black people—women especially—face today. They want to look like us but, at the same time, push the agenda that we must look like them to be beautiful.

Men and women are afraid to wear their hair in its natural state because it is perceived as dirty, unkempt, unprofessional, ghetto, etc. Many Black people have lost opportunities simply because of the color of their skin or the nature of their hair. The world keeps talking about loving yourself and at the same time criticizes us for being ourselves and tries to change us into what they have declared beauty to be.

It is only now that we are seeing some form of inclusivity in the beauty industry in things like having a foundation for all skin tones, but is that enough? We are told that each baby step is still a step in the right direction, but why should we accept small, gradual steps toward "change"? Why should we settle for breadcrumbs? There have always been different shades of people since the beginning of time, so why is that that Black people should accept slow change when we have been on earth for the same amount of time as every other race?

We have been conditioned to take whatever we can and not complain, but that isn't right. There has to be some form of justice somewhere—if not for us, then for our children. The rise of social media has made it easier for beauty standards to be enforced upon us. Everywhere you look, there is an advert or influencer who meets the accepted standard. Everywhere you look, there is a White person getting more recognition than a Black person simply because they fit the mold.

More and more people are suffering from mental health challenges because of this. The world has painted a picture depicting beauty, but we are not in it. Children are being bullied in schools, adults are being bullied online, and everywhere you look, there is someone being bullied for their looks.

For far too long, Black people have had to apologize for their looks. We have had to apologize for not have small noses or light enough skin or small enough lips or straight enough hair. We have always been apologetic for being ourselves, for looking the way we do. But why?

Black people have always been told they are too much. We have always been forced to comply with the system, to conform to the beauty standard. We are criticized for looking the way we do, and yet White people can tan their skin, fill their lips, and all sorts of other procedures to give them Black features, and the world praises them for being beautiful and trendy.

Did you know that numerous Black people in corporate America changed their names and their looks just so they could be employed? Did you know that many employers will not hire someone with a "typical Black name"? And if by some stroke of luck you manage to even get a foot through the door, you have to fit the European beauty standard just to be taken seriously.

The media and the beauty industry continue to fail Black women especially. They continually push their agendas that propagate ignorance and racism, and most of us don't even notice it. For example, how often do you see a dark-skinned woman of color on the cover of a beauty magazine? How often do you see dark-skinned women on a list of most beautiful women or faces? I'm specifically talking about women because men are not held to these same standards. In fact, dark-skinned men are now the "in" thing. More women are intrigued and attracted to darker or "chocolate-skinned" men than ever before. This does not mean that darker-skinned men have it easy, but they have it better than women.

We see it everywhere, in movies, in printed media, on social media that Black women are not beautiful. Even in the Black community, women with Eurocentric features are considered as beautiful. Our communities have been brainwashed into believing these lies too, which begs the question, Why is beauty everything that we are not?

I love the statement "Beauty is in the eye of the beholder" because it encapsulates what beauty actually is. Everyone is beautiful in their own right. What one person sees as beautiful may not be the same as another, but the important thing is to recognize that we are different and allow us to flourish in our differences.

We are more than the color of our skin or the texture of our hair. This does not make us inferior in any way. In fact, we shouldn't have to wear weaves unless we want to. We shouldn't have to feel like we're not good enough unless our hips are narrow and our stomachs are flat. We shouldn't have to feel like we're not good enough because our skin is darker or our hair is kinkier. We should be allowed the freedom to express and celebrate our individuality without judgment or prejudice.

Our bodies are perfect just the way they are, and it is time that the world accepts that. We shouldn't have to demand apologies from companies who still use racist advertisement strategies. We shouldn't have to demand larger clothing sizes or a wider range of makeup to match our skin tones. We shouldn't have to wear weaves, wigs, or perm our hair to look professional. We shouldn't have to demand things that everyone else receives freely as a right. We shouldn't have to change who we are to make everyone around us comfortable.

One of the greatest forms of oppression Black people have experienced in mental. We have been oppressed for far too long that we no longer see the beauty in ourselves. We no longer recognize how diverse we are within our race and why that is extraordinary. We have allowed this to go on for far too long because we are afraid to challenge the systems; we are afraid to stand up for ourselves and not only demand but effect actual change. We have been too comfortable accepting the bare minimum and expecting people who don't look like us to make these changes for us.

It is time that we stop relying on the white-washed media to tell us what we should look like. It is time that we take the power back into our own hands and effect the change that we want to see. We cannot keep demanding change from those who don't look like us. The power continues to be in their hands because we have allowed it. We have become too complacent with the scraps that we are given under the guise of change and inclusivity.

We are all beautiful in every shade, shape, and size, and we should not leave it up to the world to tell us what we should and shouldn't look like. We should live on our terms and look the way we want to whenever we want to.

We can no longer allow the world to try to make us White just to make them comfortable. We can no longer allow the media to tell us what is and isn't beautiful. We can no longer sit back and allow non-Black people to tell us what we should look like.

All of us need to take a stand and send a clear message that we are not White, we are Black, and we are beautiful.

Chapter 3

I Am Not a Criminal
Raising Black Men in America

Being Black makes me a crime.

This is a statement that is the unfortunate reality for Black men in America. Since the days of slavery, our blackness has been viewed as a negative thing. The one thing we cannot control is the very thing that is unacceptable.

As a mother of eight beautiful biracial children who are Puerto Rican and Black, I worry for the safety of my children every single day. We live in a society where being Black garners disgusted or fearful looks. A society where we are judged by the color of our skin and not the content of our character—to paraphrase Martin Luther King Jr.—an ugly society that is filled with hatred for their fellow man just because of pigmentation.

Our young Black men cannot walk down a street without people being suspicious or afraid of them. Black men have been living the reality of being labeled criminals before they can ever think of or actually commit one. We have a justice system that awaits our young men with open arms, a system that patiently waits for the day when it can lock away another one of our own, and that day is every single day. Crime is a crime and should be duly punished, but we are the only ones who get punished.

Studies and statistics have shown that Black men receive a harsher sentence in comparison to Caucasian men who committed the same crime. Black people are the most incarcerated race in America followed by Hispanics. And what's worse is that the system is not lenient to people of color. Just take a look at the NAACP Criminal Justice fact sheet on the next page.

NAACP Criminal Justice Fact Sheet[1]

Many of us live this reality every single day. We have fathers, husbands, brothers, friends, neighbors, cousins, boyfriends living away their years in prison. We have a vast amount of potential going to waste behind iron bars because the system is not designed to protect or correct as it should be, it is designed to keep us away, remove us from society entirely to make others feel more comfortable.

Incarceration Trends in America
- Between 1980 and 2015, the number of people incarcerated in America increased from roughly 500,000 to over 2.2 million.
- Today, the United States makes up about 5% of the world's population and has 21% of the world's prisoners.
- 1 in every 37 adults in the United States, or 2.7% of the adult population, is under some form of correctional supervision.

---

[1] Fact sheet taken from and property of https://www.naacp.org/criminal-justice-fact-sheet/.

Racial Disparities in Incarceration
- In 2014, African Americans constituted 2.3 million, or 34 percent, of the total 6.8 million correctional population.
- African Americans are incarcerated at more than five times the rate of Whites.
- The imprisonment rate for African American women is twice that of White women.
- Nationwide, African American children represent 32 percent of children who are arrested, 42 percent of children who are detained, and 52 percent of children whose cases are judicially waived to criminal court.
- Though African Americans and Hispanics make up approximately 32 percent of the US population, they comprised 56 percent of all incarcerated people in 2015.
- If African Americans and Hispanics were incarcerated at the same rates as Whites, prison and jail populations would decline by almost 40 percent.

Drug Sentencing Disparities
- In the 2015 National Survey on Drug Use and Health, about seventeen million Whites and four million African Americans reported having used an illicit drug within the last month.

- African Americans and Whites use drugs at similar rates, but the imprisonment rate of African Americans for drug charges is almost six times that of Whites.
- African Americans represent 12.5 percent of illicit drug users, but 29 percent of those arrested for drug offenses and 33 percent of those incarcerated in state facilities for drug offenses.

Effects of Incarceration

- A criminal record can reduce the likelihood of a callback or job offer by nearly 50 percent. The negative impact of a criminal record is twice as large for African American applicants.
- Infectious diseases are highly concentrated in corrections facilities: 15 percent of jail inmates and 22 percent of prisoners—compared to 5 percent of the general population—reported ever having tuberculosis, hepatitis B and C, HIV/AIDS, or other STDs.
- In 2012 alone, the United States spent nearly $81 billion on corrections.
- Spending on prisons and jails has increased at triple the rate of spending on pre-K-12 public education in the last thirty years.

If Black men are not locked away behind bars, they are wrongfully murdered.

The police—these are people who are trained to enforce the law and protect citizens…all except Black people. For the past ten years, stories of unarmed young Black men being murdered has become the norm. In fact, this has been the norm since slavery began. But now, we have newspapers, news and radio stations, every form of media has flooded us with the latest stories of the latest victims, but still, the perpetrators walk free because violence against a Black man is self-defense, but violence against a White man is violence punishable by law.

There's always a "good reason" as to why police fired the shots, but that reason has never been true. Even when our men are murdered in plain sight like Jemel Roberson, Robert Lawrence White, Trayvon Martin, Jordan Baker, Eric Garner, Jerame Reid, Gregory Gunn, and many more. Most of their murderers were acquitted, why? Because they created the system; therefore, they make it work for them. Even with stark evidence to prove that these Black men were wrongfully killed, the perpetrators are walking free because they "thought" the man had a weapon or they "thought" the man looked suspicious or they "thought" the man was violent. So many men have lost their lives to these hate crimes under the pretense of assumption.

When did being Black become a crime? When did being Black equal suspicion? When did being Black make us bad people? Where is this freedom we were promised? Where is this freedom politicians claim we all have?

So many stereotypes govern the way Black men, in particular, are perceived. None of which are true. Black men are not criminals. Black men are not ugly. Black men are not incompetent. Black men are not Black men are strong, cultured, responsible, intelligent, driven, and so much more, which is the truth that needs to be communicated. Black men have so much to offer the world if they can only be given the chance to thrive. We shouldn't have to lose ourselves or change our names just to be accepted; we should be accepted because we are human. We are citizens of the world. We are citizens of America.

Chapter 4

I Am Not a SlaveEqual Pay

Climbing the corporate ladder is no easy feat for the average person, but add being Black to that, and you have a mountain that is nearly impossible to climb. History has proven that we have been disadvantaged from the beginning. Formal education is only but a dream for the majority of the Black community. Lack of resources and financing are issues that have plagued us for generations. We have been set up for failure before any of us can even begin. Those of us who are lucky enough to make it have to work twice as hard as our Caucasian counterparts just to be recognized. And those of us who make it far enough to be accepted in the most influential circles have to set aside our blackness and conform to the standard. The education system is designed to keep us out from the beginning. We struggle with overcrowded schools and little resources as well as a shortage of teachers because most are not willing to work in these underprivileged or "high-risk" areas, not to mention the lack of extracurricular activities. You see, the disadvantage doesn't start in the job market or tertiary institutions, but it starts at the primary level, which results in children having no hope or ambition for their future because they are told and showed that they cannot achieve more than the system allows, which is nothing. Finishing high school is a dream that many Black families never get to realize. Those of us that do make it are saddled with endless student loans and lower opportunities. The employment hierarchy has always favored everyone else before us. Even now, in a time of women empowerment and equality, Caucasian females are given precedence over Black females when it comes to employment. Even in an area where we should be given equality, we still come in the last place. It is no secret that the few Black people who have truly made it and are paving the way have been exceptional individuals: former president Barack Obama, the most decorated athlete Allyson Felix, legendary rapper Jay-Z, iconic performer Beyoncé, the greatest performer of all time, the late Michael Jackson. These and many more have been exceptional people in their field. They had to work very hard and very smart, inserting themselves in spaces they "don't belong," and proving beyond a reasonable doubt that they are indeed exceptional and worthy. While we celebrate Black excellence demonstrated by these people, it is still an issue that it is only a handful of them. There are so many more intelligent, talented, hardworking Black men and women out there who might never succeed the way these icons have. Why? Because the system was not created for us to thrive. It's like beginning a race two-hundred-meter behind the star athlete.

Unfortunately, Black people still face discrimination when it comes to remuneration.

Chapter 5

I Am Worthy of Love Too Black Love Needs to Be Celebrated

Reality television is beloved by all. It keeps us engrossed and entertained all the while being relatable. But have you ever watched a reality dating show and wondered why the Black woman is never chosen or given a fair shot? This is just one example of how the media plays a hand in people's perceptions of Black people. More often than not, we are not given a fighting chance because we do not fit into the beauty standard. Racial bias and stereotypes are real even though many refuse to acknowledge it (this also stems from White privilege). It is a fact that when they see us, they don't see beauty. In a country that prides itself on being the most racially diverse, a country that is having more and more mixed-race relationships and children, Black people are still at the brunt of racial discrimination. What's worse is that a lot of Black people are giving into these biases as well. We have Black people looking down on Black people, feeding into the false narrative that we are not good enough. There's nothing wrong with dating outside your race, but there's nothing right about looking down on your own race.

We need more positive examples of Black love in the media and our communities. Black people are also capable of having happy, healthy, mature relationships. We are capable of

It is always a beautiful thing to witness Black love. It is more than a relationship but a shared cultural experience. There is nothing as comforting as being in a relationship with someone who understands you, someone you don't have to explain yourself too, someone who can relate to you on a deeper level.

The media has always tried to depict Black relationships as dysfunctional or abusive or unsuccessful when the truth is that it is perhaps could be one of the greatest experiences one can have as a Black person. This isn't to say that there aren't abusive relationships among Black people, but it is to say that Black people are capable of love and respect.

Black love means strength, compassion, principle. It is a beautiful and unique experience that is based on a shared history. It is a cultured and spiritual experience that cannot be duplicated.

If you were to ask anyone from a different race whose partner is of the same race, they, too, will tell you that there is nothing like dating within your race because there is an unspoken understanding and respect that stems from a deep generational foundation. Again, I reiterate that there is absolutely nothing wrong with interracial relationships; in fact, they are a beautiful sight to behold when two cultures come together with mutual respect and acceptance of one another.

Look at how "Black Lives Matter" began. This power statement was us taking back the power and saying enough is enough. We were tired of losing our young men to police brutality and watching the perpetrators walking scot-free, and yet that made some people uncomfortable enough to start saying, "All lives matter."

This is just one example of how we have been disregarded by society because it makes others uncomfortable. Even something as important as human life, because it is Black human life, it is watered down and made unimportant. This is the society we live in, and this is why we have to preserve our culture as well and prove that Black people can love too.

Despite popular opinion, Black men can be faithful. In fact, everyone has the ability to be faithful, but it has absolutely nothing to do with the color of your skin. Cheating is a choice, not a racial characteristic, but too many people have placed that label on Black men in particular.

Black women, on the other hand, are depicted as crazy. We are spirited and strong, but the world translates that as crazy, and the unfortunate truth is that a lot of Black men choose women of other races as life partners because they think this too. But Black women are fiercely loyal and passionate about protecting their partner and family.

Sadly, we have too many Black men abandoning their Black partners and opting for someone of a different race when they become successful. But why? Because they have fed into the narrative that Black women are not good enough or beautiful enough or even intelligent enough, and that couldn't be further from the truth. It is important to provide a reference point for future generations. We can create these positive relationships that they will look up to and emulate, but that begins with teaching our children that Black love is beautiful. It begins with us setting examples of healthy Black relationships and how successful they can be. We cannot continue to allow the media to paint us in a bad light or tell us what we can and cannot be.

This means that we need to start changing the kind of media we consume as well as creating more opportunities to showcase Black love because we cannot rely on an age-old system that is fundamentally White to dictate such an important aspect of Black culture.

Black Panther was one of the biggest movies in 2018. This is the movie that arguably had the greatest impact on the world in terms of Black culture. Not only did it showcase positive relationships, but it also showed the world that Black women are strong too. This movie made history. Black people everywhere finally saw a superhero who looks like them with dark skin, kinky hair, and a strong sense of loyalty and responsibility to his people.

All this comes down to representation. We live in the social media age, so representation matters. When we turn or our TVs or shop online, do we see people that look like us?

The ability to love another stems from the ability to love ourselves. Now more than ever, we need to learn how to love ourselves. We cannot trust the media or the education system or anything else because if we can do this, we will open up boundless opportunities for ourselves and one another. Loving ourselves will free us from the oppression of self-hatred and doubt and enable us to achieve more than we could have ever imagined.

You see, Black love is not only about romantic relationships, but it is also about loving and celebrating who we are. We have lived in oppression for far too long that we do not recognize the beauty within ourselves and each other. We need to transform our minds and not only embrace our blackness but showcase it for the world to see because that is the only way that we will free ourselves.

We can no longer allow our identity to be diluted by allowing Black people to be poorly portrayed, falsely accused, or just excluded. One of the proudest moments for me as a mother was hearing that Tyler Perry had opened his own studio. This was not only a milestone for Mr. Perry but the Black community at large because this meant that Black people would not be in control of the narrative; this meant that we could tell our truth unapologetically.

This meant that more young Black people would be given opportunities that never existed for us before, but most of all, this meant that we could finally just be Black.

Change is not a far-fetched concept, but we have to learn to love ourselves in our own skin. We don't need to bleach our skin or wear weaves (though there's nothing wrong with that) to be loved and accepted. Black love is so many things, but most of all, it is self-love.

Chapter 6

I Am Not Angry The Color of My Skin and the Tone of My Voice Don't Mean I'm Angry

"You're too loud," they said. "Relax," they said. "Why are you so angry?" "It's not that serious." These and many other patronizing words have been spoken to Black people everywhere. For generations, we have been told to lower our voices or to just keep quiet because we sound angry. As a mother, I have had to teach my boys how to respond in confrontational situations, especially those involving White people or the police. It breaks my heart that in order to protect them, I have to dim their light. If you are a parent, you can relate to this. Our deepest fear of living in

America as people of color is that our sons may not come home at the end of the day. We live in deep fear of them losing their lives at any point in time no matter how old they are.

Black people everywhere are naturally expressive. I don't know if it is in our genes or a general cultural trait, but we are. This is often interpreted as aggressive by society. We are often told to speak softer or to not react because it makes those around us feel uncomfortable.

So we need to ask ourselves a very serious question, "Why is your discomfort my problem?"

Why aren't we allowed to express ourselves the way we see fit? Why isn't it okay for us to be loud and boisterous? Why is that interpreted as anger? But more importantly, why is it reported as anger?

If you look at the hierarchy of human beings, especially from the time of slavery, Black women have always been at the very bottom. I'm sure you've heard the phrase "Angry Black woman" before. Who hasn't? It is a phrase that has been used to describe us when we express ourselves in a dominant manner or just express ourselves at all. So many Black women are afraid of expressing their opinions because that label would shortly follow if they do.

This goes back to history where White slave owners set the narrative that Black people were aggressive and should be treated as animals. That narrative is still alive today, except it doesn't have physical but mental implications now. Black men and women are afraid to speak up in the face of injustice because they know that they risk losing their jobs or their reputation; after all, someone somewhere will label them as angry.

We were raised to not be vocal but to just be grateful to be in the room, but times have changed. We are not puppets who live and move at the hands of a puppet master, but we are people with our own voices and opinions, and they deserve to be heard. We can no longer allow injustice to reign under the fist of fear.

There was a story that made headlines a few years ago that I'm sure you heard of, and that is Serena Williams demanding an apology from the umpire. Her "outburst" was nothing unseen or unheard of in a spirited sports competition, and yet she was fined $17,000 and labeled "an angry Black woman" for defending herself from cheating allegations.

History has proven time and time again that we are unfairly judged for having emotions. How many times has a Black person fallen victim to the manipulative tears of a White person who felt threatened or harassed by the said Black person who merely expressed their feelings?

Black people are forced to tone themselves down and refrain from expressing themselves. The system was created to keep us quiet, and if we don't, the real issues are ignored and a spotlight is shone on our "threatening behavior."

Now if you've been alive long enough, then at some point in time, you have either experienced or witnessed a White person bursting out in anger and getting their way. I can vividly remember one incident I witnessed.

You know how busy morning can be, especially in a coffee shop, so one day, we were all patiently waiting in line for our orders when a White man who had been frantically tapping his foot, might I add, proceeded to yell at the poor barista for wasting his time. He caused such a scene that the manager came out and forced the barista to apologize and thereafter offered the White man a complimentary coffee.

This was absolutely ridiculous and infuriating because the rest of us had to stay in the line while the man sauntered off with a free coffee in hand. At that moment, I imagined myself having a similar outburst and what the ramifications of my actions would be.

The truth of the matter is that the cops would have been called, and I would have been arrested.

This is the unfortunate reality of the society we live in. We cannot express ourselves without facing severe consequences, such as imprisonment, false allegations, or damaging labels to our reputation. One would think that at least the rich and famous would be an exception, but that's not the case. As long as you are Black, no amount of status or money can make you immune from this stereotype.

If you're like me and you love browsing through comment sections on social media to get people's general opinions, then I'm sure you've come across numerous comments of people calling on Black celebrities to say or do something. Oftentimes, these celebrities are labeled as sell-outs for their silence, but have you ever wondered why they keep silent?

Of course, not standing up for your community when you have the influence to do so is unjustifiable, and I will never try to justify it because I don't believe it's right, but I can look at the reasoning behind such behavior.

One of the unfortunate things about Black people climbing up the social ladder is that most of them conform to the status quo, and because they conform and integrate so well in the upper-class world, they assume that it makes them immune from Black issues and stereotypes. But it has been proven multiple times that those at the top are never truly accepted because one wrong move gets you out.

All Black people need to realize that being "accepted" into the White community will never make you one of them. We can love each other and embrace each other's cultures and live in a peaceful, integrated society, but at the end of the day, you are Black, and that means you risk losing everything if you fall out of step.

This does not mean that we should become racist and segregate other races, especially White people. No. This means that we need to begin to stand up for one another and fight for what is right. We have to stop allowing people to degrade and defame us for exercising our right to freedom of speech and expression. How many men have been killed for simply asking a police officer why they were pulled over? How many men have lost their lives because someone took one look at their skin and assumed they were dangerous?

Being Black does not make us angry. Being loud and expressive should be perceived as how it would be from any other race. Our skin should not automatically constitute danger.

We are not ill-mannered or unsophisticated because we have an opinion. We are not what society says we are. As a matter of fact, we are a large part of society; therefore, our voice matters too. We should be able to express ourselves freely and not teach our children, especially our young boys, to quietly cooperate when they are unjustly detained. We should have rights just like everyone else to stand up for ourselves, and we shouldn't have to lose our lives or our reputation for it.

Chapter 7

I Am More Than Just My Skin (Part 1) What Colorism Does to Us as a Community

We talk about racism and discrimination from other races and cultures, but what about the discrimination between ourselves? People say that colorism is a made-up thing by Black people as a reason to complain, but is it really real? *Colorism*, as defined by the *Merriam-Webster Dictionary*, is "prejudice or discrimination especially within a racial or ethnic group favoring people with lighter skin over those with darker skin." What does this look like in the real world? This goes back to beauty standards that are that the closer one is to White, the more attractive and less threatening they are. Colorism is just another facet of racism, but unfortunately, it exists among us as Black people too.

We all know that colorism is real, especially from ethnicities with lighter skin tones. We watch how they accept those of a lighter shade and maybe even consider them to be beautiful.

The real problem we face when it comes to colorism is that this form of segregation has filtered into the Black community too. It is no secret that Black men and women with a lighter skin tone are considered more attractive than men and women with a darker skin tone.

It is obvious in a society where a light-skinned Black man or woman is more likely to get hired than a dark-skinned man or woman. This isn't just about what is considered as attractive, but darker-skinned Black people are considered to be more threatening too.

It is painfully apparent that the closer you are to White, the more you are accepted by society. Until recent years, the Black people who were given jobs in the media were light-skinned. Sitcoms had the token Black person who was light-skinned more often than not.

Of course, being light-skinned does not take away from their Black experience, but it is no secret that lighter-skinned Black people do have it a little easier. This experience can further be dissected to separate dark-skinned men from women.

How many A-list Black actors and actresses do we have? A handful probably. And out of that handful, how many are dark-skinned? These are the issues that we need to tackle. It is not enough to demand inclusion and be satisfied when those of us closer to White are included.

Lupita Nyong'o is a talented dark-skinned A-list actress. Even with her status and accolades, she still faces harsh criticism for her looks with some going as far as likening her to apes. But if Lupita was lighter-skinned, she would have been praised for her "exotic" beauty. Now see if you can name at least five other A-list actresses with a similar skin tone to Lupita.

Is it appalling enough that there isn't enough Black representation in the media, but we also don't have enough dark-skinned representation? Dark skin has been devalued so much that aspiring actors and actresses are turned away because there is no "demand" for them, but the demand has always been there: Black people want to see fellow Black people of their TV screens. There are popular reality dating shows such as *The Bachelor* that a lot of Black people would enjoy but don't bother watching because they are barely represented.

The problem with colorism within the Black community is that it divides us. We begin to look at lighter-skinned Black people as the gold standard of what we should be. Sadly, there is also a lot of bullying based on skin tone in our community.

Colorism is similar to racism in that the effects are the same. Those with a lighter skin tone are thought of as beautiful and are automatically accepted, whereas those with darker skin tones are segregated.

It has become a plague on the Black community in which it has further damaged the self-esteem of many people and caused them to do drastic things such as bleaching their skin. We have seen many Black people bleach their skin including celebrities. This is a serious matter because it publicly shows the inner struggle that so many Black people face.

A case of someone who completely changed their looks is the late Michael Jackson. Everyone witnessed how he gradually changed his features until he could not anymore. He was a victim of racism and colorism, and that damaged his mental health.

Even though Michael was loved by millions of people around the world, he didn't love himself, and that was the issue.

There are a lot of young people growing up believing they're ugly because society says they are; some even experience these scathing remarks from family members and close friends, which is why we cannot ignore it any longer. Colorism is a problem that needs to be stopped in its tracks before it escalates any further.

A family friend of mine rushed to me for advice on how to help her son who was being bullied at school because of his dark skin tone; the little boy was bullied by fellow Black students. His mother was at her wit's end. She had tried all she could by reporting it to the principal and hiring a therapist, but the damage was so deep that the little boy tried to commit suicide.

We cannot fight oppression if it is living and breeding between us as the Black community. This story is just one of many that you will hear in your community. There many more severe cases, such as students being doused in bleach and other heinous acts. We have to put a stop to the hate that is so rampant in our community. We have to educate our children and one another and learn to accept each other;

otherwise, the world will never accept us. We cannot accuse others of the very hate that we have for one another.

I once asked a Black woman in an interracial relationship why she had married outside her race. I expected the standard answers of "love" or "he's my soulmate," but the answer she gave broke my heart. She said that she married outside her race so that her children wouldn't have dark skin like her own. She shared the struggles she had faced from school all the way into her adult life, and that was the reasoning behind her marrying a White man.

Now most people would judge her and maybe even ostracize her, but I understood her. Even though I don't agree with her reasoning, I couldn't judge her because I know just how evil colorism is. The woman could not change her own skin tone, but she could make sure her children did not go through what she went through.

This is contradictory to Black love, and that is a problem. We want the world to understand that Black people come in all shades, shapes, and sizes, and yet we refuse to accept that ourselves.

We have to stop buying into the lie that we have to be lighter in order to be accepted. Colorism is a grave distraction from what is really going on, and that's racism. We are so caught up in oppressing one another that we are fast removing our focus on the oppression we are experiencing as a collective.

So much can be said about colorism and its effects on the Black community, but the bottom line is that it is slowly killing our people; it is turning us against each other in a time when we need to band together and fight for our rights.

We are Black. All of us. It doesn't matter what shade our skin is. We are Black. The world doesn't see us as different shades. It sees us Black. We have to stop being deceived by the little acceptance a few of us receive and look at the bigger picture. We are stronger together.

Colorism is a tool to divide and distract us, but it cannot prevail if we do not feed into it. We have to fight for one another, not against each other.

Chapter 8

I Am More Than Just My Skin (Part 2) The Color of My Skin Does Not Make Me Less Intelligent

Have you ever been talked down to? Or has someone ever spoken in a slow patronizing voice to "help you understand"? How frustrating is it to be treated as though you lack intelligence?

The story of how Oprah Winfrey became the successful Black woman she is today is one that has inspired us all. She broke down barriers and stood in the face of oppression, successfully paving the way from many young Black men and women to break through the tall iron gates of television.

Oprah began her journey as an ambitious young Black woman with a high level of determination and thirst for success. She encountered many naysayers and experienced the ugly face of racism because she was a Black woman in the White-dominated world of daytime television.

Throughout her career, Oprah had to constantly prove that she was intelligent and that she deserved to be where she was. The unfortunate truth is that even after she has lived a full life and achieved so much, there are some people out there who still believe that she does not deserve everything she worked so hard to attain.

This is a problem that a lot of us Black folk face even to this day. We work hard and go to school just like everyone else with hopes of a better life, only to arrive at this said life and being told that we don't deserve it.

Black people already have to deal with having to work twice as hard as our White counterparts in order to achieve the same thing. We always have to go above and beyond to prove that we deserve what we have achieved, and that is a problem in itself.

For the first time in history (2019), Miss USA, Miss Teen USA, Miss World, and Miss Universe are all Black women. This is something that continues to be celebrated worldwide. I find it both incredible and sad. I look at how long these competitions have been around and how long ago slavery was abolished, and yet this is the first time that Black women have won all these major competitions.

Speaking of Miss Universe, Zozibini Tunzi from South Africa, she changed the face of pageantry and made history with her win. If you don't know who she is, you'll be shocked when you Google her and see a picture of a gorgeous Black woman with short natural hair and a fade. That's right, a fade.

Her win was one that got the world talking, both good and bad. She was criticized for her hair, her dark skin, and her country of origin. Some thought she was not intelligent enough to hold the title, something that she has proven to be completely false.

The point is, we, as a whole, do not have the privilege of just being celebrated for our achievements. Every little thing we do is scrutinized, and every decision we make is questioned as though we do not have the ability to make intelligent decisions. Not only is this behavior insulting, but it is degrading.

Even when it comes to job interviews, Black people have to really prove that they are intelligent and competent enough to be hired, including those that received education from the best institutions. Every rag-to-riches story in the Black community details how the person worked harder than everyone else and experienced great disappointment before finally breaking through. Why is it this way?

We have to continue saying it louder for the people at the back: the color of our skin does not make us less intelligent than everyone else.

It is deeply saddening that in a land where we are supposedly free, we have to continually prove that we deserve to be here. It is 2020, but we still have to jump through hoops just to get a foot through the door.

I bring this back to Mr. Tyler Perry and his incredible accomplishment. We all see his great success today, but many don't know that he started from nothing, pouring his heart and soul and every penny he had into writing and producing a play with hopes of a packed audience, only to be greeted by empty seats.

Of course, he only went up from there and is now the proud founder and owner of Tyler Perry Studios, but my point here is that if you ask Mr. Perry what people said to him and thought of him when he had nothing, you will probably be shocked at the number of stories he can tell. Some of those stories probably involve people looking down on him because of the color of his skin or thinking he was not intelligent enough to make it.

All these people are true examples of Black excellence, but it is not limited to them. The drive that these people possess is inherent, but that isn't the case for the majority of the Black community. We have been beaten down by the negativity of others so much so that we now doubt ourselves and our abilities.

People like Tyler Perry, Oprah Winfrey, and Zozibini Tunzi have shown us that we don't have to be anything other than ourselves, and we don't have to bend to oppression or measure our intelligence according to the standards set by society.

We are just as human as everyone else and just as intelligent and capable of achieving great things. When we believe the negative words that are spoken to us, we plant seeds of doubt in our minds. These seeds cause us to talk ourselves out of becoming what we want to because we've been told that it cannot be done.

Black people have proven time and time again that we are intelligent and creative. I mean, just look at the recent scandals in the media of White people stealing ideas of Black people and passing them off as their own.

If you want further proof, look at how our culture has been stolen and diluted. The way we dress is considered as "ghetto," and yet so many other races dress the same way and pass it off as being cool. Our music, which was once a deeply cultural thing, has now been made mainstream and changed to fit the narrative that is comfortable for all those who are now a part of it.

When you think of it, Black culture is everywhere. It is so rich, unique, and intelligent that is was stolen and transformed into something we cannot recognize. That same Black culture is what has made other races millionaires. Our culture is what has made many famous, and yet we are still stuck where we began.

When Black people finally rise and make it, the industries put us against each other so that we fail. They play mind games and work on our intelligence so that we drag each other down, and they don't have to, and the ones who have figured this out get silenced.

We are intelligent beings who deserve to reap the harvest of what we have sown. We deserve to enjoy the fruit of our culture and not stand by as mere spectators while others benefit from who we are.

We are capable of so much more than we give ourselves credit for, and all it takes to unlock the greatness within us is to shut out the negative voices of oppression and apply our minds to what we want to achieve.

Chapter 9

I Am a Citizen Too
Black People Deserve Equal
Right and Opportunities

In the first chapter, I gave a brief history of slavery in America and what that did to us as a people. In this brief history, I mentioned the amendments that enable our freedom, but I also mentioned the laws that separated Black people and White people, popularly known as "Jim Crow" laws.

As mentioned, these laws separated us from White people in every aspect, including education, transportation, employment, transportation, etc. So these laws gave power to segregation that should have been abolished along with slavery.

We face the same challenges today than we did back then and ask the same questions that we did back then: If we are citizens, why aren't we treated with equality?

This goes back to everything that has been said in this book. We are citizens of the United States of America; therefore, we deserve to be treated as such. We deserve equal rights and opportunities as everyone else. We deserve to be treated as human beings.

We are treated as though we are in a mass correctional program where one mistake immediately takes you out; one wrong move and the system basically makes it impossible for us to enjoy our full rights as citizens.

Let's start with education. The standard of public education in Black communities is dismal at best. Our schools are not equipped well enough to equip our children for a better future. If we want a better education for our children, we have to break our backs in order to afford better schools, which shouldn't be the case. Education is a right and should be treated as such for Black people too.

Next, we talk about employment. The job market is very small for Black people. A lot of us are not educated and, therefore, only hold jobs that involve manual labor, specialized skills (such as plumbing), or minimum wage jobs. The reality for many Americans is that we have to work more than one job just to make ends meet, whereas people who received tertiary education can live a balanced life working their nine-to-five.

As I mentioned earlier, those of us who are lucky enough to get a tertiary qualification are saddled with student loans that we spend most of our lives paying back. So you see that the system was designed to work against us from the very beginning.

All we want, African-Americans, is a fair shot. We want to be treated as citizens of this country. We want to walk freely down the street without fear of being shot. We want to send our children to better schools and set them up for a better life. We want better health-care services in our communities. We want to be treated fairly by the justice system.

There are so many things that we want that we don't have. All these things and more are what we should be enjoying as citizens because it is our right. We shouldn't have to beg for these things or struggle and protest just to be heard.

Equal rights and opportunities should be for all including us. The Jim Crow laws have to truly be abolished from the system. All the barriers that have been put in place to stifle our progress have to be removed. We should no longer accept being treated as secondhand when we are supposed to be first-class.

I know that it is impossible for us all to become wealthy, but we can all be successful in our own right. We can all live happy and wholesome lives. We can all live in peace and harmony with one another because there are more than enough resources to go around.

We want hate to fall and love to conquer as we build a better future for all the citizens of America, but that cannot happen if some are treated as citizens and others are locked out. Fair treatment is not an impossible task to achieve; we are all human beings who are capable of living together, empathizing with one another, and helping each other.

We are already becoming a blended society with every passing year. In fact, scientists predict that the next generation will almost all be mixed race. How will the laws operate then? How will the laws segregate when America is completely mixed?

We can begin to effect change now and embrace one another with our differences. We are all citizens of America—citizens who shouldn't have to fight one another to attain what we are all promised.

America is said to be for all; therefore, it should be for all.

Chapter 10

Black Lives Matter

This chapter is dedicated to all those who lost their lives because someone felt unjustly threatened by the color of their skin.

This is for those who lost their lives because of someone's racial bias.

This is for those who lost their lives because of someone's privilege.

Terrance Franklin
Ariane McCree
Miles Hall
William Green
Samuel David Mallard
Kwame "KK" Jones
De'von Bailey

Christopher Whitfield
Anthony Hill
Eric Logan
Jamarion Robinson
Gregory Hill Jr.
JaQuavion Slaton
Ryan Twyman
Brandon Webber
Jimmy Atchison
Willie McCoy
Emantic "EJ" Fitzgerald Bradford Jr.
D'ettrick Griffin
Jemel Roberson
DeAndre Ballard
Botham Shem Jean
Robert Lawrence White
Anthony Lamar Smith
Ramarley Graham
Manuel Loggins Jr.
Trayvon Martin
Wendell Allen
Kendrec McDade
Larry Jackson Jr.
Jonathan Ferrell
Jordan Baker
Victor White III

Dontre Hamilton
Eric Garner
John Crawford III
Michael Brown
Ezell Ford
Dante Parker
Kajieme Powell
Laquan McDonald
Akai Gurley
Tamir Rice
Rumain Brisbon
Jerame Reid
Charly Keunang
Tony Robinson
Walter Scott
Freddie Gray
Brendon Glenn
Samuel DuBose
Christian Taylor
Jamar Clark
Mario Woods
Quintonio LeGrier
Gregory Gunn
Akiel Denkins
Alton Sterling
Philando Castile

Terrence Sterling
Terence Crutcher
Keith Lamont Scott
Alfred Olango
Jordan Edwards
Stephon Clark
Danny Ray Thomas
DeJuan Guillory
Patrick Harmon
Jonathan Hart
Maurice Granton
Julius Johnson
Jamee Johnson
Michael Dean
George Floyd

And this is for us who remain.
Black lives matter. Our lives matter.

About the Author

Kierra Saddler was born and raised in Lawton, Oklahoma. She has always been a business entrepreneur while keeping up with heartbreaking events taken place in the world. She wrote this book because she was filled with so many torn emotions an understood how being Black or biracial affects herself and others in the world we live in. Kierra is a mother of eight wonderful children and a wife of an amazing, talented husband that participates in all her brilliant ideas and ventures. Kierra enjoys living in Texas now and has adapted to city life. Her journey as an author has been one of many memories she won't forget as she looks forward to being a best seller.

CPSIA information can be obtained
at www.ICGtesting.com
Printed in the USA
LVHW030137100221
678884LV00007B/667